Dance, Girl

"It's Your Life"

Dance, Girl
"It's Your Life"

Desiree Fleming

EJF Publishing House
Chicago, Illinois

Copyright © 2021 by Desiree Fleming

All rights reserved. No part of this publication may be reproduced, distributed, or transmitted in any form or by any means, without prior written permission.

Desiree Fleming/EJF Publishing House

Publisher's Note: This is a work of nonfiction. Names, characters, places, and incidents are a product of the author's imagination. Locales and public names are sometimes used for atmospheric purposes. Any resemblance to actual people, living or dead, or to businesses, companies, events, institutions, or locales is completely coincidental.

Dance, Girl "It's Your Life"/Desiree Fleming. -- 1st ed.
ISBN 978-0-9841797-9-4

DANCE, GIRL *"IT'S YOUR LIFE"*

Dance Class
Contents

Introduction..........................11

Dance, Girl 101.............................. 15

Slide, Girl 102 21

Freestyle, Girl 103.......................... 31

Step, Girl 104 39

Breakdance, Girl 105....................... 51

DANCE, GIRL *"IT'S YOUR LIFE"*

Special Dedication

I dedicate this book to my daughter, Elisa.
You are my favorite dancer and beautiful flower.
Sweetheart, your dance is so pure and brings a smile to my face and heart.
Your dance is more than motion, it is the heartbeat of your soul.
I love your creativity for it brings a fresh breath of life.
Throughout life things and people will change, but never allow it to change you.
Keep your dance, baby girl, for it is your smile!
Share your dance, darling, for it rejuvenates the weak.
Never be afraid to reinvent your dance for you hold the power to change.

Love, Mommy

DANCE, GIRL *"IT'S YOUR LIFE"*

Introduction

"Dance, Girl" is written to inspire and empower mothers, grandmothers, daughters, aunts, nieces, and granddaughters, to find their dance. Each one of us has a dance deep down inside which can light up the world around you. Whether you see it or not, you best believe me others do.

With everything women face in life, we need something to keep us going. I call this our *dance*. It is that inspiration, tenacity, and inner strength which pushes us to keep going, even when we want to stop and give up. Your *dance girl* is that inner voice which gently whispers, "Keep living, girl, don't give up, and don't lower your standards." It truly is our inspiration.

Even our little girls and teenagers deal with pressures. Sometimes, these can be more challenging mentally than what we experience as adults. When they experience situations or issues such as insecurities, broken friendships or relationships, girl arguments, they often are unaware of how to best pick up the broken pieces and get back into the swing of things. That's why having encouragement to keep dancing, even when things don't go the way they'd hoped, planned, or wished is so **important** and **imperative.**

Your smile, tears, laughter, comeback, education, career, art, vision, aspiration, style, victory, success, voice, choice . . . you fill in the blank, that is your *dance*. Allow me to share with you some different dance moves to keep you dancing, even when life gets challenging. If you're like me, you probably have found it difficult at times to just enjoy everyday life. Sometimes, the challenges we face can knock us down so hard. However, *when you realize that your purpose on this earth is greater than your opposition, you will begin to enjoy every single day of your life.* Today, you can choose to dance in the face of opposition.

Desiree

Desiree Fleming

Dance, Girl
"It's Your Right! It's Your Life!"

Can you hear the music playing?
Do you feel the yearning for freedom?
Can you sense the healing rain?
Will you dare to dance?
Will you dare to be free?
Feel the ground beneath your feet.
Let the rhythm of peace be your beat.
There's something erupting in your spirit.
Setting you free from misery.
As you dance there is no limit.
Dance, girl, soar in the Spirit.
Dance, girl, this is your release!
Dance, girl, this is your healing!
Dance girl, this is your time!
Dance, girl, it's your time to shine!
Dance, girl
It's your right
Dance, girl!
IT'S YOUR LIFE!

Written by Desiree Fleming

DANCE, GIRL *"IT'S YOUR LIFE"*

Dance
"Move Effortlessly"

The word dance is a verb, meaning to have a rhythm when one is moving. I use the term *dance* as a metaphor for how we engage everyday life. On any given day there is something to make us smile or make us sad. What do you choose? To smile or to cry? It is up to each of us to enjoy everyday life so I'm sure hoping it would be to smile. Unfortunately, situations do arise from time to time which make us feel as if we were at the bottom. It's during those "bottom" times that I want to encourage you to d*ance, girl.* Just imagine what life would be if you could d*ance* every day?

Truly, dancing is one of the most powerful open demonstrations of what one is feeling. Imagine for a moment the intimate exchange of a slow dance. The guy caresses her back and she rests her head on his chest or shoulder. Emotions rise within when you are in such close proximity to the man you love. In that moment, a couple may enjoy intimacy and freedom as if nobody else or anything else in the room.

On the other hand, there are dances which express a sense of freedom and excitement as individuals move exuberantly around the dance floor. Just think of a line or group dance. Those who know or want to learn the technique enter the dance floor and promptly join right in. Novices watch the more seasoned dancers and imitate them, trying to get the dance just right.

Are you brave enough to get on the dance floor of life and enjoy it? Is there something you enjoy doing that most people would be rather surprised to learn about you? I believe most people have something they enjoy in private when nobody is watching or that they only share with their inner circle. Have you ever just wanted to walk on a beach barefoot, wear a bikini, get a tattoo, wear a weave, eat at an expensive restaurant, go on vacation with your girls, go to a matinee on your day off work, kiss your guy in the movies, hold hands with your guy as you walk, build a snowman, run in the rain without a raincoat or umbrella? If you answered yes to any of these you have a *dance girl* inside of you that just wants to live and enjoy life. Wouldn't that be so wonderful if you could just be true to who you are everyday? Laugh when no one else is laughing or sing when no one else is singing? What are some things that are keeping you from just enjoying everyday life? What is keeping you off the dance floor of your life? Break free from it and get ready to dance.

There are many things I enjoy. I love writing, doing makeup for others, and dancing. They all satisfy me and bring a sense of peace, laughter, and fulfillment to my life. However, at those times when I feel overwhelmed by the struggles of life, I lose sight of my freedom to enjoy life. It is at those times that I am most tempted to give up. But I have learned that it is just at those moments that you have to "take lemons and make lemonade." There is no need to wallow in a crisis every day.

How wonderful it is to find ways to really enjoy life. I think of my experiences when writing which I find extremely stimulating and refreshing. Often, I get lost in creating characters for stage plays, writing short stories for children, and inspiring and empowering writings for others. When I create characters for my plays, ideas usually emerge from something funny. I laugh as if I can see it *LIVE*. When I write about sad moments, I sigh a little. I've heard that writing is therapeutic. I must say, I agree. You really can get lost in your own world while writing.

Trying my hand at makeup is also fun for me. I embrace the opportunity to be a *nonprofessional* makeup artist who produces professional looks. I can't even put into words just how exhilarating it is to choose eye color pallets, foundation, lipstick, mascara and blush. I love helping to enhance a young woman's self-confidence and appearance as she heads out to her high school prom or down the aisle at her wedding.

Lastly, my absolutely favorite thing to do is dance. I have discovered that dancing does something for my soul--it makes me feel alive! It energizes, motivates, and rejuvenates me. That is why I am always the one looking for the music whenever my family gets together to celebrate birthdays, barbeques, or graduation parties. Since I love to dance, I totally enjoy having a good DJ (disk jockey) around.

Although, I am not a professional dancer, nor have I taken any dance classes, the passion for dance pulses in my soul. Many people might be surprised to know just how much. If I could dance all day, I probably would. Well, maybe not *all* day. When I work out, I find that putting dance music in my ears energizes my tired body especially on days I need that extra push. In some ways, dancing seems to almost redeem me.

Interestingly, my daughter, Elisa has a similar passion. As soon as music comes on, she gets to moving, dancing as if nothing or no one else matters. Years ago now, I came to a realization as I watched her dance with feet tapping and body swaying. I realized that this is how I need to live and enjoy my life. In that moment, she was just having a good time, not focused on any cares or stresses. There's a freedom child enjoy as they live in the moment that we can learn from. They remind us to enjoy life each day because it is precious. Tomorrow is never promised.

Do you ever feel it's impossible to live a life of freedom and peace? I am here to say that it is possible. As women we deal with so many challenges that at times life can feel meaningless and even void. This kind of thinking has a lot to do with our mindset. But, we have to make a conscious decision to change the way we think and operate in life, even allowing ourselves to get to the point of dancing. Whether you are a mother, grandmother, or teenager, life is so much better when you can smile, laugh, and enjoy your life. So many things going on around you may push you to mope, feel sorry for yourself, get in a funk, but staying there only brings on a depressing lifestyle. Who really wants to live like that? To be honest, that's not living, that's merely existing. To exist isn't how God plans for us to live. Living is making time to smell the beautiful flowers, enjoy your children and grands, date your husband, vacation, and take walks in the park. I am a firm believer, and I have learned from experience that we choose how we live. Will you choose to dance, no matter what?

Just think, no matter which age or stage we are in life, we all have a dance within our souls. A dance that pushes or pulls you to the dance floor of life. Have you noticed how a baby bounces on your knee when music is playing? Something about the music stimulates their minds and little bodies. What happens to you when your favorite song comes on the radio? Do you pat your feet or start moving your head from side to side? Dancing is like medicine to your bones. Play something up tempo to change your mood, if it's low. Get up and dance, girl! Let the mindset of dancing become your mantra for how you live your life. Don't allow your current dilemma to stop your *inner girl* from enjoying today, tomorrow, and your future.

Slide, Girl
"Just move"

Dance techniques vary across the world. Some have different speeds and sequential steps to follow. Many cultures have their own dance styles. Interestingly, some people are so gifted that regardless of background and nationality, they can dance to almost any style of music they hear, whether they are professional dancers or not.

As much as I enjoy dancing, sometimes there are different styles of dances and techniques that I cannot do. Some are fun, but sometimes challenging. Yet for some, once they get the beat, they are able to get right in step with any of the techniques. As a matter of fact, there are a few dances you might have heard about, seen, or even participated in like the "*slide*." This is a dance where a group of individuals enter the dance floor dancing in a uniformed fashion. In the *"freestyle,"* people can do whatever they desire, within reason. "*Stepping*," yet another organized dance is more so for two individuals. Lastly, there is the *"break dance"* where individuals get all the way down on the floor to dance. Each of these dances is unique with its own place and style of music.

"Black Women are Angry"

I often hear that **"black women are angry."** Sometimes we are! Just think of the many unnecessary stresses some black women are forced to carry. I can't speak on behalf of every African American woman, but from what I have experienced and noticed, I know there are times when women have had to assume the role of husband as provider and duo parenting roles. There are instances when our husbands are so broken down emotionally and economically, women are forced to just take over and handle the home and family affairs. Then there are divorced and single mothers who are saddled with the sole responsibility of parenting. I especially feel for our single mothers who have to single handedly take care of the daily cleaning, cooking, shopping, discipline, parent-teacher meetings, and sports activities because they are doing it all on their own.

Sidebar: Single mom if the father is helping try to let go of your anger and you all work on co-parenting, the child should come first.

Women are faced with so many struggles. We have marital issues, parenting issues, friendship issues, employment issues, body type issues, mental issues, and financial issues. You name it and we've dealt with it!

I remember when my dad, who raised me from birth, took gravely ill. My young mom, who was already caring for eleven children, was forced to assume every area he always took care of. From grocery shopping, to cooking, to disciplining us, she had to make sure the bills were paid so we could keep our home. In addition to caring for her children, she now had to bathe, feed, and clothe my dad and take him back and forth to the hospital.

Did she look or seem angry? To be honest, I don't ever remember hearing her complain about it, not even once. But some of her responses to us, her children, would indicate her anger and frustration. You could sense her withdrawal and sadness. I believe what she was experiencing was like a "slap in the face." As you continue reading you'll understand.

I have a very attractive mother. Her smile was beautiful and bright. I am told I look a lot like her in her earlier years. My mom seriously had a body as gorgeous as a model. You think Beyonce has a body? My mom's body was just like hers, even after giving birth to twelve children.

Can you imagine being a young mother raising eleven children and having to care for your husband who bought your pretty young self your first home? A husband who while he was able to work made sure the family had nice cars. But, this same man was a drunk. He beat you in front of the kids and sometimes outside in front of your neighbors. He dragged, cussed out, and humiliated you. Then one day after a disagreement, he storms into the house, stands on a chair in front of his little boys and little girls, and grabs a loaded gun from a secret opening in the wall. Unbeknownst to the children, he goes to the bedroom and shoots at you. He chases after you, locking the kids in the house behind steel gates where nobody could get in or out. In broad daylight he pursues you as you try to get away. He shoots while you try to pull out of your driveway. Realizing all she was dealing with, what do you think her heart was really like? In my observation, it was shattered, broken, hurt, and humiliated.

Just look at the news. I believe in every single culture there are women dealing with domestic abuse. They are dealing with anger for one reason or another. We all share pains of loss, abuse, dysfunctions, lack, education, careers, successes, relationship issues, and failures, just to name a few. To single out one race to label as angry is unrealistic and unreasonable.

"Unapologetically Woman"

Women were created by God and when He sees us, he doesn't discriminate because of the color of our skins, the shapes of our bodies, the color of our eyes, or the length of our hair. When He made us, He made us amazingly remarkable. Women are His creation, the work of His hands. We are made in His image. When He made us, He took His time and placed every single detail in place. We should make no apologies for who we are. We are an astonishing work, His ultimate masterpiece. Knowing this, we can love who we are with no apologies. We are women, unapologetically!

"Tragedy that would make you want to walk off to save yourself."

I am writing to encourage "women." When we are faced with so much today, especially during this pandemic, deaths in our families, loss of employment and homes, separation, divorce, betrayal, missed opportunities, we find ourselves sliding into many different mood swings.

You may not fully understand the magnitude of abuse and pain my mother went through, neither do I. What she went through over thirty years ago, for about twelve years of her life, was tragic. Tragedy that would make you want to walk off, leave your children, and save yourself. But she never did. She would pack us up month after month and year after year and take us to my grandmother's home for safety. She never had the courage to leave permanently. It seems she didn't know or understand her own value nor the effect domestic abuse would have on all of our lives.

Girl, we may not agree with her choice to keep going back, but I'm sure we agree that pain is pain. No matter the circumstance, all of our sisters need encouragement to make the right choice for her life. We must refrain from judging and making other women feel stupid for her decisions. Do you realize the thousands, even millions of women, across the globe who are struggling in abusive relationships which are keeping them from dancing and enjoying everyday life? As women who understand pain, we have to love our sisters back to life. Let us choose today to love and help our mothers, friends, daughters, and neighbors to enjoy their lives.

"I promise, he was fine"

Remember, when I said that the abuse my dad afflicted on my mother affected his children? Well, let me speak for myself. When I was a teenager, I dated a guy who I thought truly loved me. I loved him. He was so good-looking and the girls at his high school were crazy about him and his brothers. They were like the jocks of their day. He was tall, dark, athletic, and I promise he was fine. We lived a few neighborhoods away from one another but that never stopped us from getting together. He would come visit me or I would go over to his house. We dated for a year before he started hitting me. He would punch me in my face, swinging at me like I was another dude. I still remember the day his mother said to me: "Desi, you must like that. You won't leave."

I thought, Are *you kidding? Do you think I made your son hit and beat me, ma'am? That I like it?* **WRONG**! After all these years, I am convinced that no teen girl or woman ever deserves to be hit, stabbed, humiliated, dehumanized, insulted. They do not deserve to die because of an argument or conflict.

For about two years of our worthless teen relationship, I endured being hit. I couldn't believe he hit me like I was his personal punching bag. And he continued to hurt me by cheating on me, over, and over again.

Sidebar: *To all my teen girls reading this, listen to me. If he hits you, says he's sorry, and then gives you something new, don't buy it! I promise he'll do it again. Love yourself enough to tell your parents, family, and the police. You don't deserve to die from domestic violence. I lost a sister because of domestic violence.*

God had to move some things around in my life for me to understand that I didn't have to stay with a guy who hit on me. I never knew that what I saw happen to my mother would one day become part of my journey, but it did. I never knew that a man who was supposed to love me by being kind and gentle would actually hurt me. I deserved to be treated with "Respect" and I still do, today. Moms, please, I'm begging you to save yourself, so you can save your children. When I look at what I went through as a teenager and realize how God rescued me from what could have been a tragic end, I am forever grateful to Him for saving my soul and life.

"We are not alone in our pain"

You may be in a very challenging and difficult place in your life right now. Do you feel like you are all alone and that no one could even fathom what you are experiencing? Know that we are not alone in our pain, just like we are not alone in our dance.

Girl, please hear me. The enemy of your soul wants to force you into a dark place of loneliness or abandonment. Darkness makes you feel as if you are all alone, but you are not! Many other women share your pain. Darkness may make you think that no one else understands, would believe you, or that there's no way out. Believe me, there is a way out! And when you break free, you can share your healing dance, dance of peace, dance of strength, dance of hope! Your dance will be a healing to your daughters, nieces, neighbors, sisters, colleagues, friends, and even your haters.

To *slide* back into a healthy place, free from abuse, might be difficult at first, but aren't you worth it? I say you are! Say this aloud: "**I am WORTH it**!" I must be honest. There are several steps to getting the *Slide* routine right at first. It will take time and effort to get back on the dance floor of your life, but you can. Just, don't quit!

There are so many different types of *slide* routines even if the routine looks different than anyone you've ever seen. It's okay. Just start moving. You might think you don't feel you have a right to smile or laugh anymore, but you do! Give yourself permission to enjoy your life again. I don't believe there is any pain worth carrying for the rest of your life.

Believe it or not, there are others waiting for you to get on the dance floor and *slide* your way back to life. You might feel as though you are crawling, but just keep on crawling until you can gain the strength and momentum to *slide*. Just imagine when the music playing the D.J. says over the mic: "Girl, it's time to celebrate you!" What an awesome feeling to know others are shouting for you to *dance, girl.*

This is your opportunity to dance, to laugh, to enjoy your life. It is time to embrace 'The new you." Every day, God gives us a new day, dance! Create a dance floor in your life where you can dance, dance, dance! Whether you get the routine down right or even create your own new routine. Get on the dance floor and *slide, girl*!

Freestyle, Girl
"Dance to your own beat"

The *Freestyle* dance technique has no particular order or technique. You can dance with or without music. It is the opportunity for you to dance the way you feel. There are no boundaries, no limits, so to speak, you do your own thing.

The *Freestyle* is one of my favorite dances as it is the one dance where I can fully be myself. There are no requirements to step to the left, step to the right, or jump up and down. It is just *doing me.* I enjoy dancing so much that doing a freestyle dance does something thrilling to my body and soul. Honestly, I find myself making up my own dances and having a great time whether I'm dancing alone or with my family or friends. This is my time to dance to my own beat.

"Dancing to Your Own Beat"

Dancing to your own beat is your freedom. If you are the type of person who is mostly used to doing things the way others suggest or encourage you to do, the *Freestyle* is just what you need. It is the space you create for yourself, even when others make you feel uncomfortable and intimidated at times. You have to be okay with allowing yourself to *freestyle* as you are developing, changing, maturing and coming into your own. The sad truth is when you decide to change, everybody will not agree with your change, but I promise you it's going to be alright. Free yourself right now and get ready to live.

Isn't it interesting that when you decide to make changes, whether it's in your physical appearance, education, career, or relationships, people always have something to say? I mean, what is it about you that makes them believe that their opinion or suggestion, for your life is better than your own? Sharing important things with family and friends is normal, but when they begin to rebut almost everything you share, you might need to revisit how much you are sharing. You don't want their unsolicited advice to stunt your freedom. I realize when we give them unspoken power over our lives, their power keeps you from finding your own voice and path.

I encourage you to acknowledge where you currently are. This will be the beginning of your *freestyle* dance which unleashes you to freely express yourself, let down your hair, and create your own moves.

Interestingly, my mother, sisters, nieces, my baby girl, granddaughter, and I all enjoy dancing. Although some dance a little better than the other, it truly seems like dancing is in our blood. For instance, my sister, Tammy, (who is no longer with us) could "step" like none other. The girl was so smooth. Her feet would just glide across the dance floor, sexy and all. When she danced all you could do was watch her as she demonstrated the epitome of freestyle. I loved watching her take her time and enjoy every moment. She had such class and sass on the dance floor.

I also enjoy observing my family members dance. Most of the time as soon as music comes on, especially when it's one of their favorite songs, they get to dancing. Their freedom is so liberating. It teaches and reminds me to just be free to enjoy my life, even when I'm going through a hard space. When children dance, they give you a sense of freedom. Whether music is on or not, children will dance. They can even create sounds to what they are feeling. Children are so adorable to me. So take their example to heart and embrace the *Freestyle* dance and do your own thing.

"Creating your Own Dance Floor"

Did you know you have the power to create space for a dance floor in your life? Nobody should have the power to take your dance from you. It's yours. I'm sure some may ask, "What is there to dance about?" There is so much to dance about! You can create your own celebration. Dancing shouldn't just be left to birthday parties. It is a part of life. Have you heard the saying, "It's a sad dog that won't wag its own tail"? Don't you agree? Think about it. If you don't celebrate yourself, who will?

It's so important to live the way God purposes and intends for us to live. Truthfully, I remember times when I didn't feel as free to express myself to the fullest, especially around certain individuals. Sometimes, when you broadcast so much of your business to others, they act like they have the "trump card" in your life. They project an illusion that their lives are so much better than yours. But, go figure! They have issues too! Stop letting people stop you and take over your dance floor.

I believe, when others are studying and trying to fix you, it blinds them to their own shortcomings. They forget they are human, with issues just like you. Unfortunately, when you allow them to fix 'poor little you,' you become their personal project. Anytime you give somebody that much power, you must realize that your relationship can become a contentious one which can cause you to feel stuck. When we get stuck in the rut of friendships and business relationships, we have a hard time finding our way out of that hole.

Those are invisible chains. They are not permanent but they need to be identified so that we can free ourselves from its power. Sometimes, we can clearly see what's going on with others, but fail to see the affliction in our own soul. This affliction dominates our ability to be productive.

I'm sure, as girls, we understand just how challenging relationships with friends, colleagues, and the opposite sex can be. My question is why do we stay stuck? I believe it is because we don't know how to break free.

I have a question: "Who told you it wasn't okay to be your authentic self?" Your authenticity will not look like anybody else's. I have had discussions where others would say "be real with me" even though I felt I was already being "authentic." Then I found myself struggling with someone else's perception of me. My realness was different, and that was okay. You have to be okay with being different. Every business relationship, friendship, or relationship needs diversity. Our uniqueness brings value and something different to the table. It's so sad to think that we allow unfruitful, hurtful words that are spoken over us to penetrate and dominate our lives.

Throughout the years, I have taken out my *freestyle* dance shoes whenever I have gotten excited about small changes and joys in my life. Sadly, I would soon find myself hanging them right back up after sharing my personal joys with others who didn't have the capacity to celebrate these joys with me. When I think about it, I used to give so much of myself to other people. I gave ideas, plans, time, energy, prayers and support, to people who I later realized never truly deserved it.

But I know that this is who I am and what I am called to do. So in actuality, all the seeds that I have sown are part of my *freestyle*. My *freestyle* is to help others see themselves the way God created them. It is to inspire and empower them to reach their potential, even when it looks like all hope is gone. Therefore, instead of losing my freedom of dance, I was gaining more momentum to dance to my own beat. It has taken me more than half of my life now to know that no one has the right to take my joy and dance.

Let me share this with you. When you decide to get your *freestyle* dance on, it may be hard at first especially because of all the different layers of struggles you may be dealing with relationally, economically, financially, professionally, or socially. But, girl, push through because you can't give up your dance. Those days are over. It's time to trade in your old dance shoes for some new ones that fit you, your life, your ups and downs. They will be your authentic *freestyle* dance shoes.

    Girl, this is your moment and opportunity to do your *freestyle* dance. Free yourself to be yourself. This dance is your freedom, your release, your liberty. Don't shut down or allow anyone else to shut you down, anymore. Begin to free yourself by sharing your joys. Enjoy the things in life and people you choose to enjoy. Remember, your *freestyle* dance is an expression of living life to the glory of God and dancing even when others feel, your timing is completely off. Now, go girl and *freestyle*!

DANCE, GIRL *"IT'S YOUR LIFE"*

Step, Girl
"Handle Life Situations with Grace"

In this chapter, I'm going to be a bit more transparent in order for us all to learn the art of stepping out. *Stepping* is a dance where one leads and the other follows with no resistance.

Have you ever *stepped* or watched a couple *step* before? Girl, in my opinion, *stepping* is one of the sexiest dances out there. It is a romanticized dance, where the man takes the lead. The woman has to be okay with him taking the lead in order for this dance to flow smoothly.

I smile as I write this because I still remember the time I danced with one of my male cousins who is a fabulous "stepper." He said to me, "Dang girl, you have to let me lead you."

At the time, I just knew I had *stepping* in "my pocket" so to speak. To my surprise, I didn't. I called myself looking cute, moving from left to right, front to back and was completely out of step. I've tried for years to step and allow the guy to lead, and I must be honest, I still struggle to release my ability to be led on the dance floor, and sometimes off. Leading is something I've always known how to do. Being the oldest sister, I have always had the responsibility of helping my mom with my younger siblings, at home and when we were out and about. Following, on the other hand, has been a struggle for years.

    Isn't that so symbolic of how we struggle to entrust our hands, plans, and even family to our Heavenly Father to guide us through life? For instance, when we accept Christ in our life as our Lord and Savior, we go through a process of allowing him to become the leader in our plans, choices, decisions, and every area of our lives. Unfortunately, for many of us, that is where we struggle in the "process." Have you ever found it hard to say "Yes, Lord" when He has guided you to do something totally different from what you had planned? I know, for me, saying "Yes Lord" has just seemed foreign, at times. I truly believe it's due to the lack of a real relationship between my natural father and me. This will not be a sob story though it has actually been part of my process on the journey to *stepping* with the Father.

"Who Am I?"

As a child, I grew up in a two-parent home. My dad and mother raised me and my ten siblings. All I knew was that the man married to my mother was my "Daddy." He loved me and raised me like his own daughter. He never made me feel as though I wasn't his biological daughter. I didn't know anything until a family member got involved. Still, he always treated me like his own daughter and that is how I will forever see myself. Here I was a child minding my own business enjoying life with my Daddy, Momma, sisters, and brothers when to my surprise, somebody introduced me to a new man, who was supposed to be my biological father.

Sidebar: Now, let me share something, if it ain't broke don't fix it. Mind your own business and let children find out from their parents. I struggled with my identity for years after finding out that all I knew was a lie.

So, I went from seeing my Daddy as protector and provider, to discovering that he was my "step-dad," all on a short car ride to my grandmother. Who could I trust? Were lies and distrust what I could expect in life?

That one discovery tremendously changed the course of my life. It not only affected many of my relationships as I grew up, but also my choices. I had been content with who God had blessed to be my father and I wasn't looking for another daddy. Life was good. I remember a few Christmases of beautiful gifts that lasted until I was probably in third or fourth grade. But that was before he got laid off work and got terminally ill. After that, I don't remember big Christmases, but my brothers, sisters and I still had each other.

As I was entering my teenage years my dad's illness worsened. I remember him losing so much weight and losing all his hair. By then, he could no longer walk on his own. The summer before eighth grade, he passed away. I had lost the only father I knew even though he barely showed any interest in me. Life was getting confusing. I was entering my teen years, you know how that can be.

Just imagine being without an understanding of what is or not acceptable for a young lady to expect from a male. I didn't have any male figures to give me direction. And now my single mom had to raise all eleven of us on her own. I started reaching out to my other dad for help with shoes and clothes. All my requests were always met with a pause before a kind but uncommitted "I'll see." I hated when he would say those words. I mean how or why would a father have to even contemplate helping his daughter that he had never paid child support for? He had never bought me school clothes, not even my eighth-grade graduation outfit, a gift, or flowers. He was like a broken record. I could expect that same response every single time I would call him for something. I mean that was painful. It's even painful as I look back on it at times.

"A Template for Relationships"

Remember I mentioned that my stepfather almost killed my mother? He would fight her, like she was a man. He would wake up fighting her, even shooting at her, on one occasion. Being raised in this type of home until I was a teenager, my "template" for relationships was an unhealthy one (I discussed it in the "Freestyle" section.) It seems that I had the best and worst of both worlds for a while. On one hand, I had a father who provided our family food and shelter. On the other hand, he was an abuser, beating my mother and treating her like trash. Needless to say, without a positive male example, I began making some poor decisions when it came to dating. I didn't know the first thing about dating. I did not know what it meant to be treated like a lady and not an object. And soon, I found myself in an abusive teen relationship (referred to in "Freestyle" section). I wasn't sure what it meant to be with somebody who just wanted sex instead of really caring about me. I didn't know or understand that my 15 year old self actually had any value and worth. I didn't know that I was worth waiting for. I didn't know that my "goodies" should have been put on lockdown until marriage. I wish I knew all these things back then. I thought my sexy appeal was a thin body and a nice booty.

At the same time, I was still trying to get the attention of my biological father. I wasn't very successful though. In 9th grade, I found myself pregnant at the age of 15years old. I was scared for my future. I was mad and cursing at my dad for not being there for me and I worried about how I would be able to provide for my baby financially.

I need to speak to my teenage girls, right here. You might have heard this before: "If I only knew then what I know now, I would have made better choices." Let me be the first to say, I totally agree because I have learned so many lessons the hard way. For one thing, I didn't understand that my jewels were worth saving and that at 15, I was way too young to be in a sexual relationship. As a result, I got pregnant. I became a teen mom and ended up raising my son with, my husband, a man who isn't my son's biological father. I promise you are truly worth the wait. We are burdened with baggage when we do not know our value and worth. If a guy truly wants to be in your life, he will not pressure you into having sex with him, not even oral sex.

    Well, back to what I was sharing earlier. Being the oldest girl in my family, I had many responsibilities when I was pretty young. With nine younger siblings, I was always in charge. This was a hard job, not one for a child, and I began to develop an aggressive demeanor. Parents don't always realize the pressure they put on their children, when they expect them to be an older sibling and surrogate parent. It may not be thought of as parenting but in actuality older children do end up feeling more like a parent than a sibling.

"The Baggage"

    As I got older, that same demeanor followed me onto the dance floor of life. By then, I was a mother, wife, business owner, and ministry leader. Relationally, I didn't know how to step back and allow God the room to lead me into a place of healing from the baggage I was carrying around all those years.

    As an adult, my family moved two hours away from my father. He never came out to visit me, not even when I graduated.

After going back to get my high school diploma, I remember sitting on my living room floor and crying like a baby. I cried my heart out to God. I was trying to understand why my dad, a man of God, didn't love me. I wondered what was it about me that was so wrong, so bad that he didn't want to be a part of my life? I had never done anything to him. Even as a teenager, I had tried to have a relationship with him.

    I was so wounded and the baggage from my childhood experiences made it difficult for me to forgive my biological dad for not being actively part of my life. How do you forgive someone who has never asked to be forgiven? Someone who never even acknowledged that they have wounded you? That was my struggle. I'm sure you've heard that "forgiveness isn't about the other person, it's about you." Oh, how true this is! It really is about you. You have to be willing to seriously let go in order to heal and step into a place of peace. It took me years to allow God into this area of my life to help me forgive him. At first, I didn't realize that I needed to forgive him. All I knew was that we had a superficial relationship and I didn't want that anymore.

    It is so interesting that I never understood how my relationship with my earthly father paralleled my relationship with God until the pain of rejection started hitting me in the face. Rejection is destructive and damages one's emotions, character, future, relationships, and name.

"Not alone on the Dance Floor"

I had been a born-again believer for over five years before I realized I was on a journey to discover "My Real Daddy." My crying about all I had wished my dad would have or could have done for me was the very thing that pushed me into developing a closer and more authentic relationship with my Heavenly Daddy, God the Father. I would often pray to the Lord about my pain, and I knew He was listening. He had been graciously waiting on the dance floor for me, all along. He began teaching me how to "*Step*" in healing and forgiveness gracefully. He took me by my hand and helped me release the years of pain, sadness, and shame. What a perfect and gentle Father He is. He was always there with me from day one, through every up and down I faced in my life. I was just too blind to recognize His presence.

I promise you, when I began to accept and know Him as my Daddy, I no longer looked for my earthly father to fill any voids I had or meet any needs. I realized that the scripture, "God is a Father to the fatherless and mother to the Motherless" was for me. (Psalms 27:10) That's the kind of Daddy we have.

"Join your Dance Partner"

Imagine a tall good-looking gentleman staring at you from across the room, as you freshen your powder and lips after dinner. He walks up and asks you to dance. Of course, you say "Yes."

Then he asks, "Have you ever *stepped* before.?"

"No" you reply.

In response, he assures you, "All I need to do is trust me. I will lead and show you the way."

Stepping alone is not that fun. But when you have a partner leading you, it is such a wonderful experience. You just glide you across the floor effortlessly. You no longer have to take charge or think about what to do next. His hand just leads you in the direction you should go.

You may be one struggling with daddy-daughter, mother-daughter, spouse, or sibling issues that are overwhelming you. Whatever you are currently dealing with, just know that it's not worth sacrificing your happiness. It's time to join Daddy on the dance floor. He is a leader like none other. He will fulfill the broken areas in your life and heal the pain when He's allowed to be the gentleman. Only He can show you the steps you need to take in this life's journey.

If you're anything like the person I was or who I sometimes fall back into, let me tell you, it can be challenging. But letting your guard down and embracing a Father who truly loves you more than anyone else could is always a win-win situation. He will guide you and show you a dance that you could never imagine.

So, come on girl! Gracefully walk to the dance floor, extend your hand to the Father, and allow Him to lead you. He's ready to guide you to your place of wholeness. Allow God to be your daddy and then *Step*, girl!

I cannot close this chapter without acknowledging how God has since healed my relationship with my father. We have had the awesome opportunity of getting to know and appreciate one another. I have discovered we have so much in common both in our personalities and our work in ministry.

Today, I do not hold anything against my dad. I love him so much and appreciate the love God shows me through him. It is my pleasure to talk to my dad almost every day. I love hearing him say that he loves me. And I especially appreciate that even at seventy years old, he texts me.

Forgiveness looks different for everyone. For me, it was embracing the fact that he is my father. It was allowing God to heal me of the hurt of my past. I realized that I loved my dad and wanted to have a relationship with him before he passed away.

Some people struggle to let go and forgive because the anger or pain is too devasting. I totally understand. I want to encourage you to consider the following if you will.

What is the benefit to you of forgiving someone? Is it helpful to relive the same pain repeatedly? Remember, everyone's choice of forgiveness may look different. Your forgiveness may be forgiving, releasing, and not having any contact with the individual. Or you may be willing to take baby steps of opening small pieces of your heart, one day at a time. But remember you will have to lean on God through this process. It can be difficult and short-lived without the help of our Heavenly Father. Yet, it is so worth it for your own benefit. Unforgiveness is like an acid, destroying the container it is stored in. You can protect yourself and save your soul by choosing to forgive. Today is a good day to make that decision.

Desiree Fleming

DANCE, GIRL 105

Breakdance, Girl
"Being Strategic in your life"

Growing up in the 1980's was amazing! I am talking paisley clothes, big hair, big shoulder pads, big pants, and guys carrying around huge boom boxes. Dancing and music was everything in that time. Rap was hitting an all-time high. Musicians battling for bragging rights, pop locking and hip hop were all on the rise. So was breakdancing. *Breakdancing* was the dance capturing the hearts of many youth. It was popular in America and around the world. Truth be told, many still enjoy doing it today.

Wow! I really am dating myself on this one. I still remember when guys and girls would *breakdance*. This was a dance where individuals would do dances on their backs and even their heads. You would see guys carrying cardboard boxes to dance on and big boom boxes to play the music. I tell you, they were breaking it down.

Breakdancing always seemed to draw crowds of spectators. Everyone wanted to see what was going down on the dance floor. In the neighborhood where I grew up, several guys always drew a crowd, but there was this one guy in particular that everybody wanted to see. He could do the snake and pop lock (figuratively throwing his chest in and out as if his heart was coming out of his chest.) He always wowed the crowd.

This dance was so strategic. Not everyone could do this dance. It took a certain kind of skill set to accomplish these moves. I mean, one could actually throw his back out, break his neck, or suffer major issues with their hands, if he didn't know what he was doing.

"Divorce Is Like Death"

In this chapter, I want to share about the art of strategically getting back on your feet after divorce. You may ask, "How in the world do I get back up, after being down for so long?"

I've heard people say **"divorce is like death."** The separation of the couple not only hurts the couple, it also hurts the children. It is the tragic loss of someone you once loved so much and never imagined life without.

Typically, divorce is a permanent breakup, without any intentions of reconciling and getting back together although in some cases couples have reconciled.

Approaching this subject is new for me since I am not divorced and never have been. But I have associates and family members who have gone through this process and I've seen firsthand the pain and struggle it brings to families. I have also seen how many have survived and come out as overcomers.

Truthfully speaking, divorce is rampant in our society. It occurs not only among non-Christians. It has become an epidemic in our Christian culture as well. I am a married Christian woman and I too have found myself at the brink of separation and having discussions of divorce.

I believe people would be surprised if they knew all the struggles that many "Christian" married partners have and are having. If we told the truth, these couples also deal with arguments, financial challenges, lack of communication, and even lack of intimacy.

Perhaps, if we are honest, we could get the help and healing we truly need. Although we desire for our marriages to reflect the relationship of Jesus and the church, there isn't any marriage on this earth that was made in heaven. No matter how good someone else's relationship looks, marriage always takes work.

Now that divorce is also rampant in the Christian community, some doubt God because of the pain it brings. Let's not blame God for our pains. Sometimes people marry for the wrong reasons. Other times individuals bring compulsive behaviors such as cheating, flirting, mental, physical, and emotional abuse into their marriages. These behaviors make it challenging to stay in a relationship when there is a breach in the "covenant relationship" between the husband and wife.

Whether it's the man or woman inflicting the abuse on the other, there needs to be healthy intervention. You might ask, "How would you know what I'm experiencing since you've never been divorced?" You're right, I may not know, but God knows the pain, loneliness, and grief you're experiencing. I promise you, He doesn't get joy or pleasure watching you break down, He wants to Heal you, are you ready.

"Breaking the Silence"

When break-dancers start off, they don't start down on the floor. They are first standing. You too were standing before the life of separation or divorce occurred. There are many women who can't explain why their husbands just walked off and left them. You are stronger than you believe, you have made it this far, don't give up now.

Breaking the silence of your pain is a necessary and healthy move. Having pent up frustration can cause certain illnesses in your body. You deserve to live better than that. Wouldn't you agree? So what if he paid all the bills and you didn't have a job? You have skills and potential. You can go back to school to learn something that will allow you to get a job to take care of yourself and your children. Know you can do it! Nobody should have that much control over your life.

Girl, don't let it break you. It's time for you to break the silence of your hidden pain and start getting back into the swing of things. You feel like there possibly isn't any way out, but truly there is. Seek wise counsel and keep it moving.

The Bible says that Jesus is acquainted with grief, there is no pain that he can't feel or heal. (Isaiah 53:3)

"The Blame Game"

Part of your healing is refusing to play the "blame game." The blame game isn't fair to either of you. One of the main reasons for staying mentally stuck in failed relationships is primarily because we can never get over who was at fault.

The blame game keeps you talking about everything negative about your ex or possibly soon to be ex-spouse. As we all know, negativity breeds confusion, disgust, gossip, frustration, and many other negative attributes.

In order to achieve your purpose in life, it is imperative that you choose to stop talking about the problem with every breath. It's doing nothing but sucking the life out of you. Regardless of whose fault it was, you need to break out to breakthrough.

Some women are good at sharing in great detail all that's going on or has gone on in their lives. But after all that sharing, that "good talk" or "good cry," I promise the pain still finds a way to resurface.

There were seasons in my marriage, when I was going through challenging times. I shared just about everything I was going through with friends. It was like I had to get it out and tell somebody about it. In the moment, venting felt like it was the right thing to do. No matter how good the "pep talks" and the "heart to hearts," all the pain of what I was going through continued to resurface. However, when I stopped talking about it, it allowed me to begin to see what was really going on and move forward.

If you really want to see things change for you, you have to think about the strategies you want to put in place to help you think differently. When you think differently, you will talk differently, and be different. Also, if there are children involved, your sanity and life matters all the more. They need to see you breaking out in the midst of what you are dealing with and not breaking down.

As I said before, *breakdancing* is a strategic dance. It takes time to learn the art of what you need and what isn't necessary. Break-dancers make preparations for what they need to use when dancing.

Your breakdance isn't about you physically getting on the ground dancing, but it is about you breaking through the cycle of defeat and living as an "overcomer." I've heard it said over and over again, "Marriage isn't to make you whole." You have to be whole before, during, and even after the marriage.

Begin forgiving yourself, forgive him, forgive them, forgive God, whoever you believe let you down. Don't just say it, release them for real. This will start the beginning of your healing. Holding on to the anger, pain, and sadness is so easy. It becomes our cozy little place of comfort.

Girl, you're better than that. You deserve to treat yourself better. Love yourself by doing something different today. Even if it is just going for a walk, reading a book, writing in your journal, playing some music, getting a manicure or pedicure, do something that will put a smile in your heart and on your face. Do not keep reliving and replaying your pain in your mind. That will only set you up for more pain.

The choice is totally up to you. Have you begun strategizing and preparing what you will start doing to break dance in your life?

Every opportunity you get to laugh, do it. Every opportunity you get to dance, do it! Every opportunity you get to speak, do it!

Every time you get to smile, do it!

There's an audience waiting for you to show up with your cardboard and your big boom box.

It's time to *Breakdance, Girl!*

Published Work By Desiree

"Where Could I Take My Shame"
"The Unprotected Daughter"

"Papatha The Adventurer"
(5-Book Children's Book Series)

Unapologetically Woman
"A Woman Without Regrets Or Excuses"
(Book Collaboration & Lead Project)

Meet Willow
(Co-written with Elisa Fleming)

"Everybody Gets It Except Willow or So She Thinks"
(Co-written with Elisa Fleming)

Dance, Girl 21-Day
"Mother & Daughter Devotional"

Dance, Girl
"It's Your Life"

Twinning Twosday (Series)
"Summer Before Middle School" Spring 2021
"You're Not My Sister" Coming Spring 2022
"Eighth Grade Dance" Coming Spring 2023

God Healed Me of Stage Three Cancer

Stage Plays Written & Published By Desiree

"A Woman Without Regrets Or Excuses" (Co-written)

"Truth Is If I Told You, You Wouldn't Believe Me"

"The Unseen Son"

"That A Boy"

"Woman At The Well"

"A Broken Family"

"Family Therapy & The Coffee Café"

ABOUT THE AUTHOR

Over the past 20 years Desiree has ministered through teaching the Gospel, in addition through written and published multiple books and literature. She continues to write to empower others. Her newest empowerment is through her podcast "Coach Des Talks". Catch her latest podcast on google and apple.

DANCE, GIRL *"IT'S YOUR LIFE"*

www.ingramcontent.com/pod-product-compliance
Lightning Source LLC
Chambersburg PA
CBHW072111290426
44110CB00014B/1888